Shell Mastery

Navigating Linux Command Line and

Scripting Essentials

By

Benjamin Evans

Book Description

Unleash the Power of Your Linux System

Shell Mastery is your comprehensive guide to mastering the Linux command line interface (CLI) and the art of shell scripting. This book equips you with the knowledge and skills to navigate the depths of Linux, whether you're a seasoned pro or a curious newcomer.

Learn by Doing: A Step-by-Step Approach

Through crystal-clear explanations, hands-on exercises, and practical examples, Shell Mastery takes you on a guided journey. Each meticulously crafted chapter offers a step-by-step approach, ensuring readers of all experience levels can build their expertise at their own pace.

Inside You'll Discover:

- Command Line Foundations: Grasp the core concepts of navigating the Linux CLI, understanding shell environments, and wielding text editors for script creation.

- Command Mastery: Conquer essential file system commands, permission and ownership management, directory manipulation, file viewing and editing, process control, system information gathering, and software package management.

- Shell Scripting Demystified: Dive deep into shell scripting with comprehensive chapters on variables, input/output operations, conditional statements, loops, functions, and error handling.

- Advanced Scripting Techniques: Explore powerful topics like regular expressions for text manipulation, task automation, and system administration scripting.

- Practical Applications: Gain valuable insights from practical tips, best practices, and real-world examples that showcase the power and versatility of the Linux command line and shell scripting.

From System Admin to Scripting Guru

Whether you're a system administrator wielding the power of the command line on servers, a software developer crafting scripts to automate tasks, or a curious enthusiast eager to unlock the full potential of your Linux system, Shell Mastery is your ultimate resource. Sharpen your skills and become a confident user of the Linux command line interface.

Empower yourself. Take control. Unleash the potential of Linux with Shell Mastery as your guide!

About the Author

Writer's Bio:

 Benjamin Evans, a respected figure in the tech world, is known for his insightful commentary and analysis. With a strong educational background likely in fields such as computer science, engineering, or business, he brings a depth of knowledge to his discussions on emerging technologies and industry trends. Evans' knack for simplifying complex concepts,

coupled with his innate curiosity and passion for innovation, has established him as a go-to source for understanding the dynamics of the digital landscape. Through articles, speeches, and social media, he shares his expertise and offers valuable insights into the impact of technology on society.

Introduction

Shell Mastery: Conquer the Linux Command Line & Scripting Fundamentals - Your Gateway to Power and Efficiency

Welcome to Shell Mastery, your immersive expedition into the heart of Linux's command line interface (CLI) and the art of shell scripting. This comprehensive guide is your launchpad to unlocking the immense power and versatility of the Linux command line and scripting.

The Allure of the Command Line:

The command line interface has served as the bedrock of computing for decades, offering unparalleled control and direct access to system resources. In the Linux realm, mastering the command line isn't just a valuable skill; it's a rite of passage, a key to unlocking the operating system's full potential. Whether you're a seasoned system administrator, an aspiring programmer, or a curious enthusiast, understanding the command line is crucial for navigating the complexities of modern computing.

Your Personalized Roadmap:

Shell Mastery transcends the boundaries of a mere book. It's your personalized roadmap to command line proficiency and scripting expertise. Our approach is both comprehensive and approachable, designed to empower learners of all experience levels. Each meticulously crafted chapter fosters a holistic understanding of key concepts, reinforced by practical examples, hands-on exercises, and real-world scenarios that solidify your knowledge.

A Deep Dive Awaits:

Our expedition begins with the foundational building blocks. We'll delve into the command line environment, explore the diverse shells offered in Linux, and equip you with the skills to effectively utilize text editors for scripting purposes. This lays the groundwork for our deeper exploration of command line mastery.

Next, we'll conquer core commands and essential techniques for navigating the file system, managing permissions, manipulating files and directories, controlling processes, gathering system information, and handling software packages. We'll meticulously dissect, explain, and demonstrate each command through practical examples, ensuring a solid grasp of fundamental operations.

Once armed with a firm foundation in the basics, we'll venture into the realm of scripting. Here, we'll explore the building blocks of shell scripting, including variables, input/output operations, conditional statements, loops, functions, and error handling. Through step-by-step guidance and hands-on exercises, you'll gain the confidence to craft your own scripts.

For those seeking to push the boundaries, we offer an optional deeper dive into advanced topics such as regular expressions, automating tasks, and scripting for system administration. These chapters provide invaluable insights for readers aiming to elevate their skills to the next level.

The Power is in Your Hands:

Shell Mastery: Navigating Linux Command Line and Scripting Essentials is your trusted companion on your journey to command line proficiency and shell scripting mastery. Whether you're a beginner embarking on your Linux adventure or an experienced user seeking to expand your knowledge, this book caters to all.

So, join us on this exciting expedition into the heart of the Linux command line. With dedication, practice, and the guidance provided within these pages, you'll soon discover the limitless potential that awaits you in the realm of shell scripting. Unleash the power within – let's embark on this journey together!

TABLE OF CONTENT

Chapter 1

Unveiling the Power: Command Line and Shell

Scripting in Linux

Welcome, adventurer! This chapter marks the
beginning of your expedition into the captivating
realm of the Linux command line and shell
scripting. We'll embark on a journey to unveil
the fundamentals of this powerful interface and
explore how scripting unlocks efficiencies in the
Linux ecosystem. By the chapter's end, you'll
possess a solid foundation – understanding the

"what" and "why" of the command line, and how shell scripting empowers you to streamline tasks and automate repetitive processes.

Command Line: A Textual Portal

Imagine a world devoid of flashy icons and menus – a realm where power lies in the precision of typed commands. This is the essence of the command line, a text-based interface that grants users direct access to the heart of their Linux system. Unlike graphical user interfaces (GUIs), the command line thrives on the simplicity and efficiency of text-based instructions. This very simplicity empowers you to perform a vast array of tasks, from basic file manipulation to intricate system administration maneuvers.

The Shell: Your Command Line Interpreter

Think of the shell as your trusty translator in the command line realm. This program acts as a bridge, interpreting the commands you type and transforming them into actions your system can understand. Linux boasts a diverse selection of shells, each offering unique features and functionalities. Here's a glimpse into some popular choices:

- Bash (Bourne Again Shell): The reigning champion, Bash serves as the default shell for most Linux distributions. Its extensive feature set and adherence to POSIX standards make it a versatile and reliable choice.

- Zsh (Z Shell): For the power users, Zsh beckons with its advanced features. Auto-completion, error correction, and a vibrant plugin ecosystem elevate your command line experience to new heights.

- Fish (Friendly Interactive Shell): Embracing user-friendliness, Fish prioritizes a smooth learning curve. Syntax highlighting and autosuggestions make it an excellent choice for beginners.

Understanding the strengths of different shells empowers you to select the ideal tool for your specific needs, optimizing your command line journey.

Shell Scripting: Automating Your Workflow

The command line offers interactive control, but shell scripting unlocks a whole new level of efficiency. It allows you to automate repetitive tasks by crafting reusable scripts. Imagine a series of commands bundled into a single file – that's the essence of a shell script. Written in a scripting language (often Bash), these scripts are executed sequentially by the shell, streamlining complex tasks and ensuring consistency in system administration and software development.

Taking the First Steps:

To embark on your command line and scripting adventure, all you need is a terminal emulator. This software provides a text-based interface for interacting with the shell. Most Linux distributions come equipped with options like GNOME Terminal or Konsole. If you prefer a lighter alternative, xterm or tmux are excellent choices.

With your terminal emulator ready, you're poised to begin exploring the command line and experimenting with shell scripting. Buckle up, for the following chapters will delve deeper into the core concepts and techniques, equipping you with the knowledge and skills to navigate this powerful world with confidence.

The Adventure Begins:

This chapter has laid the foundation for your exploration. We've unveiled the command line, explored the diverse shells available in Linux, and discovered the power of shell scripting for automation. Armed with this knowledge, you're now prepared to delve into the practical aspects of command line usage and scripting in the forthcoming chapters. The journey awaits – let's unlock the potential within!

Chapter 2

Mastering Your Domain: The Linux Shell Environment

Welcome back, intrepid explorer! In this chapter, we delve deeper into the Linux shell environment, transforming you from a visitor into a master of your domain. We'll dissect its core components, unveil configuration options, and explore common features. By the chapter's end, you'll possess a thorough understanding of how the shell environment functions and how to tailor it to your unique workflow.

The Shell's Blueprint:

The Linux shell environment operates like a well-oiled machine, with several key components working in harmony to provide a seamless user experience. Let's break down these building blocks:

- The Prompt: Your Command Gateway: Imagine a blinking cursor, often accompanied by username, hostname, and directory information – that's the prompt, your gateway to issuing commands. This visual cue signifies the shell's readiness to receive your instructions.

- Shell Variables: Data Trove at Your Fingertips: Think of shell variables as named boxes storing valuable information. These can be user preferences, system settings, or temporary data. Commands like echo and export empower you to view and manipulate these data caches.

- Shell Configuration Files: The Customization Hub: Behind the scenes, shell configuration files (.bashrc and

.bash_profile for Bash) hold the key to personalization. These files, located in your home directory, are executed at each shell session startup. Here, you define aliases, set environment variables, and configure shell behavior, crafting a shell environment that reflects your preferences.

- Shell History: A Record of Your Command Adventures: The shell thoughtfully maintains a record of your past commands, accessible through your shell history. This allows you to recall and reuse commands from previous sessions, saving you time and effort. Keyboard shortcuts and utilities like history empower you to navigate and search through this valuable record.

Shaping Your Shell Experience:

The beauty of the Linux shell environment lies in its flexibility. You can customize various aspects to suit your workflow and preferences. Here are some common ways to make the shell your own:

- Aliases: Shorthand for Efficiency: Imagine replacing lengthy commands or sequences with shorter, more convenient aliases. This is the power of aliases! Define them in your shell configuration files to streamline frequently used commands. For instance, an alias named ll for ls -l simplifies listing directory contents with detailed information.

alias ll='ls -l'

- Environment Variables: Fine-Tuning the System: Environment variables function as global controls, defining the operating environment for both shell sessions and processes. Set them to manage various aspects of shell behavior, including your default editor, language settings, and search paths for executable files.

```
export EDITOR=vim
```

- Prompt Customization: A Touch of Personality: The standard shell prompt is functional, but why not add a touch of flair? Customize its appearance and behavior to display additional information or visual cues. Change the color or format, showcase your current git branch, or even display the system load average.

```
PS1='\[\e[1;32m\]\u@\h \w \$\[\e[0m\] '
```

Configuration Files: Demystifying the Magic:

Shell configuration files are the cornerstone of customization. Typically found in your home directory, these files are automatically executed when you start a new shell session. Let's explore some common ones:

- ~/.bashrc: This file kicks in for interactive non-login shells, like when you open a new terminal window. It's commonly used for defining aliases, setting environment variables, and customizing the prompt.

- ~/.bash_profile or ~/.bash_login: These files are executed for login shells, used when logging in locally or remotely.

They're ideal for setting environment variables and running commands that should only occur once per login session.

- /etc/profile: This system-wide configuration file applies to all users during login. It's used to set global environment variables and configure system-wide settings.

Chapter 3

Craft Your Scripts: Mastering Text Editors in the Linux Arena

Welcome, script architects! This chapter equips you with the essential tools for constructing powerful shell scripts – text editors. We'll delve into their role within the Linux command line, explore popular options, and unveil how to leverage them for maximum efficiency. By the chapter's end, you'll be well-versed in selecting and wielding the perfect text editor to bring your scripting visions to life.

The Text Editor's Forge:

Imagine a blank canvas where lines of code take shape – that's the essence of a text editor. Unlike word processors focused on aesthetics, text editors are designed for the raw power of text manipulation. They provide the foundation for creating, editing, and manipulating text-based files, making them the blacksmith's forge for crafting robust shell scripts in the Linux environment.

A Bounty of Editing Options:

The Linux landscape boasts a diverse array of text editors, each catering to specific preferences and skill levels. Here, we'll delve into three of the most prevalent choices:

1. Vim: The Champion's Choice: Forged in the fires of efficiency, Vim is a powerful and highly configurable text editor revered by experienced users and developers. It thrives on a modal editing system, offering distinct modes for navigation, editing, and command execution. While its initial learning curve may seem steep, its mastery grants unparalleled speed and flexibility – a true

champion's tool.

2. Emacs: The Extensible Powerhouse:
   Emacs isn't just a text editor; it's a
   customizable ecosystem. This versatile
   and extensible editor offers a vast array of
   features for editing, programming, and
   boosting productivity. Emacs Lisp, its
   built-in scripting language, empowers you
   to tailor the editor to your exact needs,
   making it a favorite among those who
   crave a highly personalized environment.

3. Nano: The Friendly Beginner's Forge: For those embarking on their scripting journey, Nano offers a welcoming gateway. This user-friendly editor prioritizes simplicity and ease of use. Its minimalistic interface and basic editing features make it an excellent choice for beginners who value a straightforward approach to text manipulation.

Optimizing Your Scripting Workflow:

The right text editor can significantly enhance your shell scripting workflow. Here are some key considerations:

- Syntax Highlighting: Imagine your code adorned with colors that illuminate its structure. Syntax highlighting, offered by most editors, differentiates between commands, variables, and comments, making your scripts easier to read and understand.

- Code Folding: Not all code needs to be constantly visible. Code folding allows you to collapse and expand sections, enabling you to focus on specific parts of your script while maintaining an organized overview.

- Automatic Indentation: Consistent formatting is crucial for code readability. Automatic indentation, a feature offered by many editors, ensures your code adheres to proper formatting conventions, enhancing readability and maintainability.

- Terminal Integration: Seamless workflow is paramount. Some editors integrate with the terminal, allowing you to execute shell commands directly from the editor window and view the output within the same interface.

A Closer Look at the Champions:

Let's take a magnified look at our three powerhouse editors:

- Vim: Vim operates in distinct modes, each with a specific purpose. Mastering these modes unlocks a world of efficiency. It offers a plethora of features, including syntax highlighting, code completion, the ability to split the editor window for side-by-side editing, and the power of macros and plugins to extend its functionality.

- Emacs: Emacs thrives on extensibility. It offers built-in support for various programming languages and editing modes. Features like syntax highlighting, code navigation, integration with version control systems, and Emacs Lisp, its powerful extension language, empower you to craft a unique editing experience.

- Nano: Nano's simplicity is its strength. While it offers basic editing features like syntax highlighting, search and replace, and line numbering, its intuitive interface and keyboard shortcuts streamline common operations for beginners.

Chapter 4

Mastering the Terrain: Essential File System

Commands

Welcome, fellow explorers! This chapter equips
you with the essential tools to navigate the vast
digital landscape of the Linux file system. We'll
delve into the commands that empower you to
traverse   directories,   manage   files,   and
manipulate their contents with precision. By the
chapter's end, you'll possess a mastery of core
file system operations, enabling you to navigate

with confidence and become a true lord of your digital domain.

Charting Your Course: Navigation Commands

Imagine the Linux file system as a sprawling kingdom, meticulously organized with directories acting as provinces and files as your valuable resources. To explore this digital realm effectively, you'll need these trusty tools:

- pwd: This command acts as your loyal mapmaker, revealing your current location within the file system. It displays the absolute path of the directory you currently occupy.

$ pwd

/home/user/documents

- cd: Think of cd as your trusty steed. Specify the desired directory path, and cd will transport you there, allowing you to swiftly move between different regions of your digital kingdom.

```
$ cd /path/to/directory
```

- ls: Envision ls as your cartographer, generating a detailed map of the current directory's contents. It displays a list of files and subdirectories, providing a comprehensive overview of what treasures lie within your current location.

```
$ ls

file1.txt  file2.txt  directory1  directory2
```

Establishing Your Domain: Managing Files and Directories

Now that you can navigate with ease, it's time to establish your dominion over your digital landscape. These powerful commands grant you the ability to create, manipulate, and organize your files and directories:

- mkdir: This command acts as your architect, constructing new directories to categorize and organize your digital domain. Specify a name, and mkdir will bring your directory to life, establishing new provinces within your kingdom.

$ mkdir new_directory

- touch: For those seeking to establish new files or breathe life into existing ones, touch is the tool. It creates new empty files or updates the timestamps of existing ones, ensuring your records are properly documented.

```
$ touch new_file.txt
```

- cp: Imagine duplicating valuable resources across your digital landscape. The cp command empowers you to copy files and directories from one location to another, ensuring information reaches all corners of your domain, creating backups, or sharing resources with your subjects.

```
$ cp file1.txt /path/to/destination
```

- mv: Sometimes, reorganization is necessary. The mv command allows you to move (or rename) files and directories, streamlining your digital infrastructure and keeping your kingdom well-organized.

```
$ mv file1.txt /new_directory
```

- rm: Wield this command with caution, for it possesses the power to erase. The rm command removes files and directories from the system. Remember, deletion is permanent, so use it judiciously to declutter your domain.

```
$ rm file1.txt
```

Unveiling the Secrets Within: Viewing File Contents

To extract the knowledge and information stored within your files, we turn to these trusty companions:

- cat: For a complete and unfiltered view of a file's contents, cat displays everything from beginning to end. Think of it as a scholar deciphering an ancient scroll, revealing the entire text of a document.

```
$ cat file1.txt
```

- less: For voluminous files, navigating line by line is essential. The less command displays the content of a file one page at a time, allowing you to explore its depths with control, just like a researcher carefully examining a lengthy manuscript.

```
$ less file1.txt
```

- head: A sneak peek is sometimes all you need. The head command displays only the first few lines of a file, providing a glimpse into its introductory content, similar to skimming the first page of a book to understand its topic.

```
$ head file1.txt
```

Guarding Your Domain: Working with File Permissions

The Linux file system prioritizes security. File permissions dictate who can access, modify, and execute files and directories. The chmod command empowers you to adjust these permissions and safeguard your digital domain:

- **chmod

Chapter 5

Safeguarding Your Domain: Permissions and Ownership

Welcome, system administrators! This chapter equips you with the knowledge to secure your digital domain. We'll delve into the concepts of permissions and ownership, the cornerstones of file system security in Linux. By understanding how to manage these aspects, you'll ensure the integrity and confidentiality of your valuable data.

Understanding File System Security:

Imagine your Linux system as a well-guarded fortress. Permissions and ownership act as the gatekeepers, controlling access to your files and directories. Three types of permissions govern this control:

- Read (r): Allows users to view the contents of a file.

- Write (w): Allows users to modify the contents of a file.

- Execute (x): Allows users to execute a file if it's a program.

These permissions apply to three entities:

- Owner: The user who created the file.

- Group: A designated group of users associated with the file.

- Others: All other users on the system.

To view the current permission settings, use the ls -l command:

$ ls -l file.txt

-rw-r--r-- 1 user group 1024 May 5 10:00 file.txt

In this example, the first set of characters (-rw-r--r--) represents the permissions. The leftmost character indicates the file type (- for a regular file). The following three characters represent the owner's permissions (rw-), the next three represent the group's (r--), and the last three represent others' (r--).

Commanding Access: Managing Permissions

The chmod command empowers you to adjust these permissions, granting or revoking access as needed. Follow the chmod command with the desired permission changes and the file or directory name:

$ chmod u+w file.txt # Grant write permission to the owner

This command adds write permission (w) for the file owner (u). Similarly, you can modify permissions for the group (g) and others (o).

Understanding Ownership: Who Holds the Keys?

Every file and directory has an owner and a group owner. The owner is typically the user who created the file, while the group owner is a designated group with associated privileges. Use the ls -l command to view ownership information:

$ ls -l file.txt

-rw-r--r-- 1 user group 1024 May 5 10:00 file.txt

Here, "user" owns the file, and "group" is the group owner.

Transferring Control: Managing Ownership

The chown command allows you to transfer ownership of files and directories. Follow chown with the new owner, a colon (:), and the new group owner, followed by the file or directory name:

```
$ chown new_owner:new_group file.txt
```

This command changes the owner of file.txt to new_owner and the group owner to new_group.

Establishing Your Outposts: Creating Directories

The mkdir command acts as your architect, constructing new directories to categorize and organize your digital domain. Specify the desired directory name following mkdir, and a new directory will be established:

$ mkdir new_directory

This command creates a new directory named new_directory in the current working directory.

Charting Your Course: Navigating Directories

The cd command serves as your trusty steed, transporting you between different regions of your digital kingdom. Specify the path of the directory you wish to navigate to after cd:

$ cd path/to/directory

This command changes the current working directory to the specified directory.

Surveying Your Domain: Listing Directory Contents

To scout the contents of a directory and identify your resources

Chapter 6

Unveiling the Secrets Within: Viewing and Editing Files

We'll explore essential commands and techniques for viewing and editing files in the Linux environment. Mastering these skills is fundamental for efficient workflow, empowering you to extract information and manipulate text-based content with precision.

Peering into the Depths: Viewing File Contents

Several trusty companions stand ready to assist you in viewing file contents:

- cat: Envision cat as a scholar deciphering an ancient scroll. It displays the entire contents of a file in an unfiltered stream, ideal for smaller files:

$ cat message.txt

- less: For voluminous files, a page-by-page approach is recommended. less acts like a magnifying glass, allowing you to examine the file one page at a time, facilitating navigation with ease:

```
$ less system.log
```

- head: Sometimes, a glimpse is all you
  need. The head command functions like a
  lighthouse, illuminating only the first few
  lines of a file, providing a quick overview
  of its introductory content:

```
$ head crontab
```

Reshaping the Landscape: Editing Files

The Linux world offers a diverse arsenal of text
editors, each catering to different preferences.
Here are a few popular choices:

- nano: For those seeking a user-friendly and approachable editor, nano is the perfect guide. Its intuitive interface makes it ideal for beginners:

```
$ nano document.txt
```

- vim: For the power users and customization enthusiasts, vim reigns supreme. This versatile editor offers a vast array of features and commands, empowering you to manipulate text with precision:

$ vim configuration.sh

- emacs: This veteran editor boasts extensive functionality and a passionate user base. While its steeper learning curve might deter newcomers, its power and customizability make it a favorite among experienced users:

$ emacs code.py

Navigating the Textual Terrain:

While exploring files within your chosen editor, you'll leverage keyboard shortcuts or built-in commands for navigation. For instance, in less, you can use the arrow keys to scroll and the j and k keys to move up and down, respectively.

Unearthing Hidden Gems: Searching within Files

Imagine searching for a specific treasure within your digital domain. The grep command acts as your metal detector, meticulously combing through files for a specified search term:

```
$ grep "error" system.log
```

This command searches for the term "error" within the system log file and displays lines containing that term.

Gauging the Activity: Viewing Processes

To gain insight into the ongoing operations within your system, the ps command acts as your trusted advisor. It displays a snapshot of currently running processes, providing details such as process ID (PID), username, and CPU usage:

```
$ ps
```

Wielding Control: Managing Processes

Your arsenal for managing processes includes these powerful tools:

- kill: This command allows you to send a signal to a specific process, enabling you to terminate it gracefully. Think of it as a gentle nudge, prompting the process to shut down:

$ kill 1234   # Send termination signal (SIGTERM) to process 1234

- killall: For more forceful measures, killall acts as a decisive commander. Specify the process name, and killall terminates all processes matching that name:

```
$ killall firefox
```

Background Operations: Working with Background and Foreground Processes

By appending an ampersand (&) to a command, you can instruct it to the command.

I see you've identified some improvements for the section on Background and Foreground Processes in Chapter 8: Process Management. Here's the updated version incorporating your feedback:

Background Operations: Working with Background and Foreground Processes

The ability to run processes in the background is a valuable feature in the Linux environment. It allows you to initiate a long-running task without blocking your terminal for its completion. To run a process in the background, simply append an ampersand (&) to the end of the command:

Bash

```
$ long_running_command &
```

This will execute the long_running_command and return you to the prompt, allowing you to continue working in the terminal while the command runs in the background. There are two ways to identify background jobs:

1. Using the jobs command: This command displays a list of all background jobs currently running in your terminal session.

2. Using the shell history: Background jobs are denoted by a percentage sign (%) followed by a job number when listed in your shell history using the up and down arrow keys.

Bringing Background Processes to the Foreground:

Once a process is running in the background, you may want to bring it back to the foreground to interact with it directly. The fg command allows you to do this. Specify the job number of the background process you want to bring to the foreground after fg:

$ fg %job_number

For example, if the job number of your background process is 1, you would use the following command:

$ fg %1

This will bring the background process with job number 1 to the foreground, suspending any currently running foreground process.

Monitoring Processes:

Several utilities provide real-time insights into running processes on your system. Here are two popular options:

- top: This classic tool displays a dynamic view of system processes, including CPU usage, memory consumption, and uptime. It provides a comprehensive overview of system resource utilization.

- htop: Similar to top, htop offers a visually appealing and interactive interface for monitoring processes. It allows you to navigate and sort process information using keyboard shortcuts.

By understanding how to manage background and foreground processes, you can streamline your workflow and efficiently utilize your terminal environment.

Chapter 7

Unveiling Your System: Essential Information

Commands

Welcome, system administrators, developers, and power users! This chapter equips you with the tools to delve into the inner workings of your Linux system. Understanding the intricacies of your hardware, resources, and network configuration empowers you to troubleshoot issues, optimize performance, and ensure system health. By mastering the commands presented here, you'll gain the ability to gather essential system information efficiently.

Peering Under the Hood: Viewing System Information

To obtain a quick overview of your system's identity, the uname and hostname commands serve as your initial guides:

- uname: Think of uname as an identification card for your system. It displays crucial details such as the kernel name, version, and underlying architecture:

```
$ uname -a
```

Linux myserver 5.10.0-11-amd64 #1 SMP Debian 5.10.92-1 (2022-01-14) x86_64 GNU/Linux

- hostname: This command reveals the system's designated network name, acting as its label on the digital landscape:

```
$ hostname
Myserver
```

Taking Inventory: Checking Hardware Information

For a more detailed examination of your system's hardware components, several tools are at your disposal:

- lscpu: This command unveils the characteristics of your central processing unit (CPU), including its architecture, core count, and threading capabilities:

```
$ lscpu
Architecture:    x86_64
CPU(s):        4
Thread(s) per core: 2
Core(s) per socket: 2
Socket(s):      1
```

- lshw: Envision lshw as a comprehensive system inventory list. This command provides detailed information about all installed hardware components, from the CPU and memory to network adapters and storage devices:

$ sudo lshw

Note: Running lshw often requires administrative privileges (sudo).

- lspci: For a focused examination of PCI (Peripheral Component Interconnect) devices, the lspci command serves as your magnifying glass. It displays a list of all PCI devices connected to your system:

```
$ lspci
```

Gauging System Health: Monitoring System Resources

Maintaining the well-being of your system requires monitoring its resource utilization. The following commands provide valuable insights:

- top: This classic tool offers a dynamic view of running processes, their CPU and memory consumption, and overall system load. Think of it as a real-time system performance dashboard:

```
$ top
```

- htop: If you prefer a more visually appealing and interactive interface for process monitoring, htop is an excellent alternative to top. It allows you to navigate and sort process information using keyboard shortcuts:

```
$ htop
```

- df: To assess disk usage and available storage space, the df command is your trusted ally. It displays information for all mounted file systems:

```
$ df -h
```

The -h flag provides human-readable output with units like gigabytes (GB) and megabytes (MB).

Charting the Network Landscape: Checking Network Information

Understanding your network configuration is essential for troubleshooting connectivity issues. These commands provide valuable insights:

- ifconfig: This traditional command displays information about network interfaces, including their IP addresses, MAC addresses, and network status:

$ ifconfig

- ip: For more advanced network configuration and troubleshooting, the ip command offers a broader feature set. It can be used to view and manage network interfaces, routing tables, and other network settings:

```
$ ip addr show
```

This knowledge empowers you to diagnose problems, optimize performance, and ensure the stability and security of your Linux system. Remember, practice using these commands and explore their options to become a proficient investigator of your digital domain.

Unveiling the Package Management Landscape

Imagine a well-stocked warehouse brimming with software components. Package managers act as your intelligent inventory control system in the Linux environment. They automate the process of installing, updating, and removing software packages, ensuring all the necessary dependencies are met. Different Linux distributions (like Ubuntu, Fedora, or Arch Linux) employ distinct package management systems, each with its own strengths and characteristics. Here are some of the common ones you'll encounter:

- APT (Advanced Package Tool): This robust system reigns supreme in Debian-based distributions like Ubuntu and Debian itself.

- YUM (Yellowdog Updater, Modified): Red Hat-based distributions such as

CentOS and Fedora traditionally leverage YUM for package management.

- DNF (Dandified YUM): As a successor to YUM, DNF offers an enhanced experience for users of newer Fedora and CentOS versions.

- Pacman: Arch Linux and its derivatives rely on Pacman, known for its speed and rolling release model.

- zypper: openSUSE and SUSE Linux Enterprise distributions utilize zypper for their package management needs.

Regardless of the specific package manager you encounter, the core principles remain remarkably consistent. Let's delve into the essential commands that empower you to manage software packages effectively.

Essential Package Management Commands:

Equipping yourself with a few fundamental commands is all it takes to become a package management pro:

- Installation: To add a new software package to your system's arsenal, use the

install command, followed by the package
name:

```
$ sudo apt install package_name   # For
APT-based systems
```

Remember, for most administrative tasks
involving package management, you'll need to
use sudo to gain temporary administrative
privileges.

- Updates: Keeping your software
  up-to-date is crucial for security and
  performance. The update and upgrade
  commands form a powerful one-two

punch:

- ○ sudo apt update refreshes the list of available packages and their latest versions.
- ○ sudo apt upgrade upgrades the installed packages on your system to their most recent versions.

- Removal: When software is no longer needed, you can remove it using either the remove or purge command:

- sudo apt remove package_name removes the package itself but keeps configuration files.

- sudo apt purge package_name eliminates both the package and its configuration files, offering a more thorough cleanup.

Maintaining Your Software Sources: Repositories

Package managers retrieve software packages from designated repositories, acting as online archives brimming with software. You can manage these repositories to fine-tune your software sources:

- Adding Repositories: To expand your software selection, you can add new repositories using specific commands depending on your package manager (e.g., sudo add-apt-repository for APT).

- Removing Repositories: If a repository is no longer needed, you can remove it by deleting the corresponding file from the designated directory (often /etc/apt/sources.list.d/ for APT).

Exploring the Nuances:

While the core concepts remain consistent, each package manager has its own set of commands and functionalities. For in-depth exploration, consult the documentation specific to your Linux distribution. Fortunately, the knowledge you gain here will provide a solid foundation for navigating any package management system you encounter.

Whether you're installing the latest development tools, system utilities, or desktop applications, package managers streamline the process. Experiment with the commands introduced here on your own system to solidify your understanding and become a confident software

manager in the Linux domain.

Chapter 8

Navigating the Network: Essential Command-Line Tools

Understanding how to diagnose, configure, and monitor network connections using the command line is a fundamental skill for network troubleshooting and maintaining system health. By the end of this chapter, you'll be wielding powerful tools to investigate network connectivity and resolve any issues that may arise.

Peeking Under the Hood: Checking Network Configuration

To gain a foundational understanding of your network configuration, the ifconfig and ip commands serve as your initial guides:

- ifconfig: Think of ifconfig as a network map for your system. It displays information about each network interface, including its IP address, MAC address (hardware identifier), and current status (active or inactive):

```
$ ifconfig
```

- ip: For a more in-depth exploration of network configuration, ip offers a broader range of features. It allows you to view and manage routing tables, network namespaces, and other advanced network settings:

```
$ ip addr show
```

Verifying Connectivity: Testing Network Reachability

Before venturing further, it's wise to confirm you can reach the outside world. The following commands act as your digital probes:

- ping: Imagine tossing a pebble across a pond; the ping command functions similarly. It sends echo requests to a specified host (like a website) and awaits a response, verifying network connectivity:

$ ping google.com

If successful, you'll see replies indicating the packets reached their destination and returned.

- traceroute: Sometimes, it's helpful to see the bigger picture. The traceroute command maps the route data packets take to reach a destination, providing valuable insights for troubleshooting connection issues:

$ traceroute google.com

By examining the hops along the path, you can identify potential bottlenecks or network congestion points.

- netcat: This versatile tool acts as a Swiss Army knife for network communication. netcat allows you to establish TCP or UDP connections to remote hosts, facilitating more advanced network debugging and exploration:

$ nc -vz google.com 80

This command attempts to open a connection to port 80 (commonly used for web traffic) on google.com, providing information about the connection status.

Demystifying DNS: Checking DNS Configuration

The Domain Name System (DNS) acts as the internet's phonebook, translating human-readable domain names (like google.com) into numerical IP addresses that computers understand. The following commands help ensure your DNS settings are functioning correctly:

- nslookup: Think of nslookup as a directory inquiry tool. You can use it to query DNS servers and see how they resolve domain names to IP addresses:

$ nslookup google.com

- dig: For a more comprehensive DNS investigation, dig offers a richer set of features. It allows you to query specific

DNS record types and gain detailed information about domain name resolution:

```
$ dig google.com
```

Keeping an Eye on Traffic: Monitoring Network Activity

Maintaining a watchful eye on network traffic is crucial for identifying potential problems and optimizing performance. These tools provide real-time insights:

- tcpdump: This command acts as a packet sniffer, capturing network traffic flowing across a designated interface. You can then examine the captured data to analyze communication patterns and identify anomalies:

```
$ sudo tcpdump -i eth0
```

- Wireshark: If you prefer a visual interface for network traffic analysis, Wireshark is an excellent graphical tool. It allows you to capture, inspect, and filter network packets, providing a user-friendly way to delve into network communication:

```
$ sudo wireshark
```

By mastering the basic networking commands presented in this chapter, you'll gain the ability to diagnose network connectivity issues, configure network settings, and monitor network activity effectively. Remember, consistent practice is key to solidifying your skills. Experiment with these commands on your system and explore their capabilities further to become a confident network navigator in the Linux environment.

What is Shell Scripting and Why Should You Care?

Shell scripting involves writing scripts, essentially sequences of commands, in a language that the shell interprets. The shell acts as a command-line interface, the bridge between you and the operating system. Common shells used for scripting include Bash (widely used and beginner-friendly), Zsh (known for its customization options), and Dash (lightweight and efficient).

So, why embrace shell scripting? Here are some compelling reasons:

- Automation Hero: Repetitive tasks become a breeze with shell scripts. Imagine automatically backing up your files or updating your system every week – scripts handle it all, saving you time and effort.

- Customization Champion: Shell scripts are like bespoke suits – tailor them to your specific needs. Whether you're managing user accounts or deploying applications, scripts can be crafted to perfectly fit your workflow.

- System Administration Savior: System administrators leverage shell scripts extensively. Tasks like user management, software installation, and configuration management become far more efficient with scripted automation.

Building Your Scripting Foundation: Basic Script Structure

Think of a well-structured script as a recipe for success. Here are the key ingredients:

1. Shebang Line (The Interpreter): The first line, often referred to as the shebang line, tells the system which shell to use for interpreting the script. For Bash scripts, it's typically #!/bin/bash.

2. Commenting Your Code (Readability is Key): Comments, denoted by the # symbol, act as explanatory notes within your script. They enhance readability and maintainability, making your scripts easier to understand for yourself and others.

3. Commands: The Workhorses: Shell scripts are all about commands! These commands can be anything from basic system utilities to file manipulation tools, variable assignments, control structures for decision-making, and function calls for

code reusability.

Data Juggling: Variables and Data Types

Variables act as storage containers within your scripts, holding data you can reference and manipulate. Bash scripting uses a simple syntax for variable definition: variable_name=value. Here are the essential data types you'll encounter:

- Strings: Textual data like greetings or file paths, always enclosed in quotes (e.g., "Hello, world!").

- Integers: Whole numbers used for calculations (e.g., 42).

- Arrays: Collections of elements you can access using an index (e.g., my_array=(element1 element2 element3)).

Taking Control: Control Structures

Control structures are the decision-making mechanisms of your scripts. They allow you to conditionally execute commands or repeat actions based on certain conditions:

- if/else: Evaluates a condition and executes specific commands based on the outcome (true or false).

if [condition]; then

```
# Commands to execute if condition is true
else
# Commands to execute if condition is false
fi
```

- for: Loops through a sequence of elements, executing commands for each item in the sequence.

```
for item in list; do
# Commands to execute for each item
done
```

- while: Continues executing commands as long as a specified condition remains true.

```
while [ condition ]; do

    # Commands to execute while condition is true

done
```

Code Reusability: Functions

Imagine having a block of code you can use repeatedly throughout your scripts. Functions provide this very functionality. Define a function with a name and the commands it executes, then call it whenever needed:

```
function_name() {

    # Commands to execute

}
```

```
# Calling the function

function_name
```

The Scripting Adventure Begins

With a grasp of variables, control structures, functions, and the overall script structure, you're well-equipped to embark on your scripting journey. Experiment with writing simple scripts to solidify your understanding and witness the power of automation firsthand. The Linux shell awaits your commands, and shell scripting empowers you to transform them into efficient workflows!

Chapter 9

Interactive Scripts: Mastering Input and Output

Understanding how to acquire user input, process arguments, and control output is paramount for building robust and user-friendly scripts in the Linux environment. By the end of this chapter, you'll be wielding techniques to transform your scripts into powerful and engaging tools.

Engaging in Dialogue: Reading User Input

Imagine your script acting as a digital assistant, prompting users for information. The read command empowers you to achieve this! It snags a line of text from standard input (typically the keyboard) and stores it in a variable you define:

```
echo "What's your name?"
read name
echo "Greetings, $name!"
```

Here, the script prompts for the user's name, stores it in the name variable, and then personalizes the greeting.

Command-Line Arguments: Tailoring Script Behavior

Scripts can be like chameleons, adapting their behavior based on user-provided arguments. These arguments, passed when you execute the script, are stored in special variables like $1 (first argument), $2 (second argument), and so on. Here's an example:

```bash
#!/bin/bash


echo "The first argument is: $1"
echo "The second argument is: $2"
```

Running this script with arguments like:

$ ./script.sh apple banana

Would result in:

The first argument is: apple

The second argument is: banana

Extracting Data from Files: Reading File Contents

Shell scripts can delve into the treasure trove of information stored in files. Standard input redirection (<) allows you to feed the contents of a file directly into your script:

```
while read line; do

  echo "Line content: $line"

done < data.txt
```

This script iterates through each line in the data.txt file, displaying each line's content on the terminal. For more granular control, you can use loops to process each line individually.

Guiding the Output: Redirection Techniques

Imagine a scenario where you want to capture a script's output for later analysis. Shell scripting offers redirection techniques to control where output goes:

- Standard Output Redirection (>): This steers the script's output to a file instead of the terminal. For example:

echo "Script Output" > output.log

Here, the echo command's output is redirected to the output.log file.

- Standard Error Redirection (2>): Sometimes, errors occur. Error redirection allows you to isolate error messages from the script's regular output, making troubleshooting more efficient:

```
cp non_existent_file destination 2> error.log
```

Any error messages generated by the cp command trying to copy a non-existent file will be captured in the error.log file.

Building Well-Rounded Scripts

By mastering the techniques explored in this chapter - reading user input, processing arguments, working with files, and controlling output - you'll elevate your shell scripting abilities. Experiment with these concepts in your own scripts. As you craft interactive experiences and manage data flow efficiently, your scripts will transform from basic tools into versatile and user-friendly companions in the Linux environment.

Conditional Statements: Scripting Decisions

Imagine a script that greets users differently based on the time of day. Conditional statements make this possible! These constructs allow your script to evaluate conditions and execute specific commands based on the outcome (true or false). The primary conditional statements are if, elif (optional for handling additional conditions), and else:

```
if [ condition ]; then
  # Commands to execute if condition is true
```

elif [another_condition]; then

   # Commands to execute if another_condition is

true

else

   # Commands to execute if none of the

conditions are true

fi

For example:

hour=$(date +%H)

if [$hour -lt 12]; then

   echo "Good Morning!"

elif [$hour -lt 17]; then

   echo "Good Afternoon!"

```
else

  echo "Good Evening!"

fi
```

This script retrieves the current hour and displays a personalized greeting based on the time.

Loops: The Power of Repetition

Sometimes, a task needs to be repeated multiple times. Loops are your secret weapon for automation! Shell scripting offers two primary loop types: for and while.

- For Loop: Perfect for iterating over a predefined sequence of elements.

```
for item in apple banana cherry; do

  echo "Processing: $item"

done
```

This loop iterates through a list of fruits, printing a message for each item.

- While Loop: Continues executing commands as long as a specific condition remains true. Ideal for situations where the number of repetitions is unknown beforehand.

```
count=0

while [ $count -lt 5 ]; do
```

```
echo "Loop Iteration: $count"

count=$((count + 1))  # Increment counter

done
```

This loop continues printing messages five times, keeping track of the current iteration using a counter.

Steering the Flow: Break and Continue

Imagine needing to exit a loop early or skip a specific iteration within a loop. break allows for premature loop termination, while continue skips the remaining part of the current iteration and moves to the next:

```
for item in files/*; do

  if [[ $item == *.bak ]]; then

    echo "Skipping backup file: $item"

    continue  # Skip processing backup files

  fi

  # Process other files

done
```

This loop iterates through files, skipping any
files with the .bak extension using continue.

Scripting Like a Pro

Conditional statements and loops are the
cornerstones of dynamic shell scripting. By
mastering these concepts, you empower your

scripts to make informed decisions, automate repetitive tasks, and adapt to changing conditions. Experiment with these techniques in your scripts to create intelligent and versatile tools that streamline your workflow and enhance your control over the Linux environment.

Chapter 10

Scripting Nirvana: Achieving Modularity with Functions

Functions transform your scripts from monolithic structures into well-organized building blocks, promoting code reusability, maintainability, and a Zen-like clarity. By the end of this chapter, you'll be a function virtuoso, composing elegant and efficient scripts.

Functions: The Bricks of Modular Scripts

Imagine a complex script as a sprawling castle. Functions act as the individual bricks, each meticulously crafted for a specific purpose. A function is a named block of code that performs a well-defined task, residing within your script. Similar to built-in commands, functions offer greater flexibility by accepting input (parameters) and returning output (values).

Building Your Function Arsenal: Definition

Defining a function is a breeze. Simply follow this syntax:

```
function_name() {
  # Commands to execute
}
```

For example:

Bash

```
greet_user() {

  echo "Welcome aboard, $1!"

}
```

This function, aptly named greet_user, personalizes a welcome message using a parameter.

Calling Upon Your Functions

To leverage a function's power, simply use its name followed by parentheses:

```
greet_user "Captain Kirk"
```

This invokes the greet_user function, passing "Captain Kirk" as the parameter.

Passing Arguments: Functions with Parameters

Functions can be like adaptable tools, taking on different behaviors based on the arguments you provide. These arguments, passed when calling the function, are accessible within the function using special variables like $1 (first argument), $2 (second argument), and so on. Here's an example:

```
calculate_area() {
  local length=$1
  local width=$2
```

```
  local area=$((length * width))

  echo "Area: $area"

}
```

calculate_area 10 5

In this example, the calculate_area function takes two arguments (length and width) and calculates the area, demonstrating the power of parameter usage.

Returning Values: Sharing Results

Functions can return values using the return statement, allowing them to communicate results back to the main script. The return value can be accessed using the $? variable after the function call:

```
get_random_number() {
  local random_number=$(shuf -i 1-100 -n 1)
  return $random_number
}


random_number=$(get_random_number)
echo "Random number: $random_number"
```

The get_random_number function generates a random number and returns it using return, which is then captured by the main script.

Local Scoping: Keeping Variables in Check

Variables declared within a function using the local keyword are private citizens, visible only within that function's scope. This prevents conflicts with variables in the main script or other functions:

```
configure_settings() {
  local username="admin"
  echo "Username (inside): $username"
}


username="default_user"
configure_settings
```

```
echo "Username (outside): $username"    #
Outputs "default_user"
```

Here, the configure_settings function has its own
username variable, separate from the one in the
main script.

Embrace Modularity

Functions are the cornerstone of modular shell
scripting. By leveraging functions, you
decompose complex scripts into manageable
blocks, promoting code reusability,
maintainability, and overall script clarity.
Incorporate functions into your scripts to craft
modular masterpieces - well-organized, efficient

tools that streamline your workflow and empower you to conquer tasks in the Linux environment.

The Debugging Toolkit: Unearthing Script Issues

Imagine a script malfunctioning – error messages erupt, and the desired outcome remains elusive. Fear not! Our debugging toolkit empowers you to pinpoint the culprit. Here are key strategies:

1. Echoes of Insight: Printing Debug Messages

Strategically placed echo or printf statements act as breadcrumbs, revealing the script's execution flow and variable values:

```bash
#!/bin/bash

# Debugging example
echo "Script initiating..."

name="Alex"
echo "Name variable: $name"

# More commands...
```

echo "Script complete."

2. X-Ray Vision: Using set -x

This command activates the shell's debugging superpower, meticulously printing each executed command, its arguments, and the exit status:

```
#!/bin/bash


# Enable x-ray vision

set -x


# Script commands...
```

Deactivate x-ray vision (optional)

set +x

3. Swift Termination: Using set -e

This command enforces strictness – any command with a non-zero exit code triggers immediate script termination, pinpointing potential errors swiftly:

#!/bin/bash

Activate error-on-failure mode

set -e

```
# Script commands...


# Deactivate error-on-failure mode (if necessary)

set +e
```

Building Script Resilience: Error Handling
Techniques

Even the most meticulously crafted scripts can
encounter errors. Error handling mechanisms
ensure your scripts respond gracefully to these
situations:

1. Exit Codes: The Universal Language of
   Errors

Commands return exit codes – 0 signifies success, while non-zero indicates an error. Utilize this information to guide your script's behavior:

```
#!/bin/bash


# Check if a file exists
if [ -f "data.txt" ]; then
  echo "File found."
else
  echo "Error: File not found." >&2  # Redirect error message
  exit 1  # Non-zero exit code for error
```

fi

2. Error Messages: Keeping Users Informed

When errors arise, informative messages displayed using echo or printf empower users to understand the issue:

```
#!/bin/bash


# Check if a file exists
if [ -f "data.txt" ]; then
  echo "File found."
else
   echo "Error: File not found." >&2  # Display
error message
```

```bash
  exit 1  # Non-zero exit code

fi
```

3. Error Logging: A Trail of Clues

Redirect error messages to a log file using >> for comprehensive error tracking and historical analysis:

```bash
#!/bin/bash


# Check if a file exists
if [ -f "data.txt" ]; then
  echo "File found."
else
  echo "Error: File not found." >&2  # Display
error message
```

```
   echo "Error: File not found. (data.txt)" >>
error.log  # Log error
   exit 1  # Non-zero exit code
fi
```

The Debugging Detective

Equipped with these skills, you can craft robust and reliable shell scripts that can weather unexpected errors and navigate challenges gracefully. Incorporate these practices into your scripts to build resilience and ensure smoother operation, solidifying your mastery of the Linux environment.

Chapter 11

Text Kung Fu: Mastering Regular Expressions

Welcome, script warriors! This chapter equips you with the art of text manipulation using regular expressions (regex) – the ultimate weapon for wielding power over text data in your shell scripts. Regular expressions are concise patterns that allow you to search, match, and transform text with incredible efficiency. By the end of this chapter, you'll be a regex master, crafting scripts that manipulate text with precision and grace.

Demystifying Regular Expressions

Imagine a cryptic code with the power to navigate through text. That's the essence of regular expressions! They consist of literal characters and special symbols (metacharacters) that represent patterns within your text data.

Breaking Down the Regex Arsenal:

- Literal Characters: These match themselves exactly in the text.

- Metacharacters: These are the special forces of regex, each with a unique mission:

- .: Matches any single character (think of it as a wildcard).

- ^: Matches the beginning of a line (like a starting flag).

- $: Matches the end of a line (like a finishing line).

- []: Matches any single character within the square brackets (like a character set).

- *: Matches zero or more occurrences of the preceding

character or group (greedy by default).

- +: Matches one or more occurrences of the preceding character or group (eager to find at least one).

- ?: Matches zero or one occurrence of the preceding character or group (non-greedy, happy with just one).

- () : Groups expressions together, allowing for complex pattern building.

•

Wielding Regex in Shell Scripting

Regular expressions are like versatile tools that can be used with various shell commands for text manipulation:

- grep: The mighty text hunter, searching for lines matching your regex pattern in files or input streams:

-

Find lines containing "error" in system.log
grep "error" system.log

- sed: The stream editor, performing in-place text transformations based on regex patterns:

Replace all occurrences of "bug" with "fixed" in bug_report.txt

```
sed 's/bug/fixed/g' bug_report.txt
```

- awk: The data-wielding warrior, extracting and manipulating specific text based on regex matches:

Print usernames from entries with a shell set to "/bin/bash" in passwd file

```
awk '$1 ~ /bash$/ {print $1}' passwd
```

Examples of Regex Fu in Action:

- Matching a Specific Word: Use the word itself as the pattern.

grep "security" config.txt

- Matching Numbers: Use [0-9]+ to match one or more digits.

grep "[0-9]+" data.csv

- Matching Email Addresses: A more complex pattern like [a-zA-Z0-9._%+-]+@[a-zA-Z0-9.-]+\.[a-zA-Z]{2,} targets email structures.

```
grep                                    -E
"[a-zA-Z0-9._%+-]+@[a-zA-Z0-9.-]+\.[a-zA-Z]
{2,}" userlist.txt
```

Mastering Text Manipulation

Regular expressions are a powerful tool for text manipulation in shell scripting. By understanding their syntax and applying them with commands like grep, sed, and awk, you can automate complex text processing tasks with ease. Experiment with different regex patterns and shell commands in your scripts to become a master of text manipulation. This will transform your scripts into versatile tools that can handle diverse text-based tasks with precision and efficiency, empowering you to conquer text-related challenges in the Linux environment.

Here's an improved version of Chapter 18: Automating Tasks with Shell Scripts:

Identifying Automation Opportunities:

The key to successful automation lies in recognizing tasks that are ideal candidates. Look for tasks that share these characteristics:

- Repetitive: Frequently performed tasks are prime targets for automation. Shell scripts can tirelessly execute these tasks with perfect consistency, freeing you for more strategic endeavors.

- Time-Consuming: Does a particular task devour your valuable time? Automating it with a shell script can significantly reduce the time it takes, allowing you to focus on other priorities.

- Prone to Error: Are there tasks where even minor human mistakes can lead to problems? Shell scripts eliminate the potential for human error, ensuring tasks are executed flawlessly every time.

Common automation targets include:

- File Backups: Safeguard your data by automating regular backups of critical directories.

- Log File Monitoring: Automate the process of monitoring log files for errors or specific events, enabling proactive issue detection.

- Software Installations: Streamline software deployment across multiple systems using automated installation scripts.

- System Maintenance: Automate routine system maintenance tasks like disk cleanup or security updates.

- Data Processing: Repetitive data processing tasks become effortless when automated with shell scripts.

Crafting Effective Shell Scripts:

Once you've identified tasks for automation, it's time to craft the shell scripts that will bring them to life. Here's a step-by-step approach:

1. Plan the Heist: Clearly define the objectives and requirements of the task. Identify the input data, processing steps, and desired output. Think of this as planning a heist – meticulous planning ensures a smooth operation.

2. Write the Code: Use a text editor to write your shell script. Incorporate commands, control structures (like loops and conditionals), and functions as needed to automate the task. Think of this as building your tools for the heist.

3. Rigorous Testing: Test your script thoroughly under various conditions and edge cases. Imagine testing your heist plan for different scenarios – you want to ensure it works flawlessly.

4. Execute and Monitor: Once tested, execute the script and monitor its output for any errors or unexpected behavior. Just

like after executing a heist, you want to review the results and ensure everything went according to plan.

Example: Automating File Backups – A Case Study

Let's explore a practical example: automating file backups using a shell script. The objective is to create a compressed backup of a specified directory and its contents.

```
#!/bin/bash


# Define source and destination directories
source_dir="/path/to/source"
```

```
backup_dir="/path/to/backup"


# Create a timestamp for the backup folder
(think unique filenames!)
timestamp=$(date +"%Y%m%d_%H%M%S")
backup_folder="backup_$timestamp"


# Create the backup directory (handle potential
errors)
mkdir -p "$backup_dir/$backup_folder" || { echo
"Error creating backup directory!" >&2; exit 1; }


# Compress and copy files to the backup
directory (be efficient!)
```

```
tar  -czf  "$backup_dir/$backup_folder.tar.gz"
"$source_dir"


echo            "Backup            completed:
$backup_dir/$backup_folder.tar.gz"
```

This shell script incorporates error handling (checking for directory creation problems) and efficiency measures (using tar for compressed backups).

Scheduling Tasks with Cron: Automation on Autopilot

Once you have your shell scripts in place, leverage cron – the time-based job scheduler in

Unix-like systems – to schedule their automatic execution. Imagine setting a timer for your automated tasks!

To schedule a task with cron, edit the crontab file using crontab -e and add a line specifying the schedule (time and date) and the command to execute. The crontab entry acts as your automated task schedule.

For instance, to schedule the backup script to run daily at 2:00 AM, you'd add the following line to the crontab:

```
0 2 * * * /path/to/backup_script.sh
```

Chapter 12

Automating the Force: Shell Scripting for

System Administration

Welcome, system administrators! Buckle up –
we're diving into the powerful world of shell
scripting for Linux administration. System
administration is the art of keeping your systems
healthy, performant, and secure. Shell scripting
equips you with the tools to automate routine

tasks, monitor system resources, and configure settings with precision. By the end of this chapter, you'll be a scripting Jedi, wielding the power of automation to streamline your workflow and become a master system administrator.

Conquering Tedium: Automating System Maintenance

System maintenance involves a never-ending stream of tasks like updating software, purging temporary files, monitoring logs, and performing backups. Shell scripts can automate these tasks, ensuring they're completed consistently and on time. Imagine a tireless droid handling these chores, freeing you for more strategic initiatives! Here's an example script automating some maintenance tasks:

```bash
#!/bin/bash


# Update package repositories (remember, keep your software fresh!)
sudo apt update


# Upgrade installed packages (security patches are essential!)
sudo apt upgrade -y
```

# Clean up unused packages and dependencies (minimize clutter!)
sudo apt autoremove -y

# Remove temporary files (keep your system tidy!)
sudo rm -rf /tmp/*

Backup your system (disaster recovery is crucial!)
(Add your preferred backup commands here)

Guarding the Gates: Monitoring System Resources

System administrators need to be vigilant about resource utilization. Shell scripts can monitor CPU usage, memory usage, disk space, and network activity. By keeping an eye on these metrics, you can identify potential bottlenecks, anticipate resource shortages, and optimize system performance. Think of it as having a real-time map of your system's health.

Here's a script showcasing some monitoring commands:

```
#!/bin/bash
```

```
# Monitor CPU usage (identify resource hogs!)
```

```
top -n 1 -b
```

Monitor memory usage (ensure enough free RAM!)
```
free -m
```

Monitor disk space (avoid running out of room!)
```
df -h
```

Monitor network activity (track incoming and outgoing traffic!)
```
iftop -n 1
```

Managing Your Minions: User Accounts and Permissions

User accounts and permissions are the gatekeepers of your system's security. Shell scripts can automate user management tasks like creating accounts, modifying user attributes, and assigning permissions. This ensures consistency and enforces security best practices across your system. Imagine managing your users with the efficiency of a droid army commander!

Here's a script demonstrating user account creation:

```
#!/bin/bash
```

```
# Create a new user account (secure with a
strong password!)
sudo useradd -m -s /bin/bash newuser


# Set a password for the new user (use a secure
password hashing mechanism!)
echo "newuser:STRONG_PASSWORD" | sudo
chpasswd  # Don't store passwords in plain text!


# Add the new user to a group (grant appropriate
permissions!)
sudo usermod -aG groupname newuser  #
Replace "groupname" with the desired group
```

Building Your Empire: Automating System Configuration

System configuration tasks like network settings, firewall rules, and service management can be tedious and error-prone. Shell scripts can automate these tasks, ensuring consistent and accurate configurations across multiple systems. Imagine deploying configurations across your systems with the precision of a starfleet engineer!

Here's a script demonstrating basic configuration automation:


```bash
#!/bin/bash
```

```
# Configure network settings (connect to the
outside world!)
sudo ip addr add 192.168.1.10/24 dev eth0
sudo ip route add default via 192.168.1.1


# Set up firewall rules (protect your system from
intruders!)
sudo ufw allow ssh
sudo ufw enable


# Manage system services (keep essential
services running!)
sudo systemctl start service_name
```

```
sudo systemctl enable service_name  # Replace
"service_name" with the desired service
```

Scripting for Efficiency and Security

Shell scripting empowers system administrators
to automate routine tasks, streamline workflows,
and improve efficiency. But remember, with
great power comes great responsibility! Always
prioritize security when scripting. Use sudo
judiciously, explore alternatives with limited
privileges, and consider testing configurations in
separate environments before deployment.
Secure your backups to prevent data loss. By
combining scripting with a security-conscious

approach, you can become a system administration Jedi Master, ensuring a well-maintained, efficient, and secure Linux environment. May the scripts be with you!

Conclusion

Congratulations, Scripting Padawan!

This book has been your guide on a thrilling quest through the realm of shell scripting for Linux. We began by unlocking the secrets of the command line, the foundation upon which all scripting is built. You wielded essential commands to navigate the digital landscape, mastered file manipulation, and harnessed the power of the shell itself. Now, you move with confidence in this text-based world.

Our journey continued as we delved into the fundamentals of shell scripting. You learned to craft your own scripts, wielding variables like tools in your scripting belt. Loops and conditionals became your loyal companions, guiding the flow of your programs. You mastered the art of input and output, ensuring your scripts interact seamlessly with the system and the user. With these core principles at your grasp, you were empowered to automate those tedious tasks that once held you back.

But the path didn't end there. We ventured further, exploring the advanced techniques that elevate a script from apprentice to master. Functions became your modules, reusable components that structure your code with elegance. Regular expressions, once cryptic symbols, transformed into powerful tools for manipulating text with precision. Error handling, your loyal shield, safeguarded your scripts from unexpected pitfalls. Now, you approach complex automation challenges with a seasoned scripter's confidence.

Finally, we put your honed skills to the test in the crucible of system administration. You learned to automate system maintenance, ensuring your systems run smoothly. Resource monitoring became an open book, allowing you to identify bottlenecks and optimize performance. User management and system configuration, once manual processes, yielded to the efficiency of scripts. By automating these tasks, you became a master of efficiency, a guardian of system health, and a champion of streamlined workflows.

Shell scripting is not just a skill; it's a superpower. For system administrators, it's a wand of automation, streamlining tasks and freeing them for strategic endeavors. For developers, it's a crafting tool, building custom solutions and enhancing workflows. For anyone who interacts with Linux, it's a key that unlocks a world of efficiency and power.

This book has equipped you with the essential knowledge and techniques to embark on your own scripting odyssey. Remember, practice is your constant companion, and experimentation is the fuel for innovation. Delve into additional resources, explore new concepts, and push the boundaries of what's possible.

As you continue your Linux adventure, may your scripts be ever elegant, your solutions ever efficient, and your automation ever powerful.

Farewell, Scripting Padawan. Go forth and script the future!

Acknowledgements

Writing a book is a collaborative effort that involves the support and contributions of many individuals and organizations. I would like to express my sincere gratitude to everyone who has been part of this journey and has contributed to the creation of this book.

First and foremost, I am grateful to the Linux and open-source community for their continuous innovation, support, and passion for sharing knowledge. Without their dedication to free and open-source software, this book would not have been possible.

I extend my heartfelt thanks to my mentors and educators who have guided and inspired me throughout my journey in learning about Linux and shell scripting. Your wisdom, expertise, and encouragement have been invaluable.

I would like to acknowledge the countless authors, developers, and contributors whose work has paved the way for the knowledge shared in this book. Your contributions to the

Linux ecosystem have enriched the lives of millions of users worldwide.

A special thank you to my family and friends for their unwavering support and understanding during the writing process. Your encouragement and belief in me have been a constant source of motivation.

Last but not least, I express my gratitude to the readers of this book. Thank you for choosing to embark on this journey with me. I hope that the knowledge and insights shared in these pages will empower you on your own Linux journey.

Thank you, everyone, for being part of this incredible adventure.

Warm regards,

Elena Sterling